# SPOOKY
# TRICKS

Weekly Reader Books presents

# SPOOKY TRICKS

by Rose Wyler and Gerald Ames
Pictures by Tālivaldis Stubis

Harper & Row, Publishers New York, Evanston, and London

An I CAN READ Book

This book is a presentation of Weekly Reader Books.
Weekly Reader Books offers book clubs for children from
preschool through junior high school.

For further information write to:
**Weekly Reader Books**
1250 Fairwood Ave.
Columbus, Ohio 43216

Weekly Reader Books offers several exciting
card and activity programs. For information,
write to WEEKLY READER BOOKS, P.O. Box 16636,
Columbus, Ohio 43216.

SPOOKY TRICKS

# CONTENTS

The night is dark
and shadows creep around.
Voices whisper in the gloom.
Listen—and shiver!
This is a night of ghosts and spooks
and scary magic.
Who will do the magic?
You will.
You will do spooky tricks
and scare everyone, even yourself.
Are you ready?

# HOW TO BE A SPOOK

## You are full of holes

Are you a real spook?
Are you full of holes
like a real spook?
Let's see.
Roll up a sheet of paper to make a tube.
This is your magic X-ray machine.
Hold up one hand beside the tube.
Look through the tube with one eye.
But keep your other eye open too.
It seems there is a hole in your hand!
There! You are a real spook.

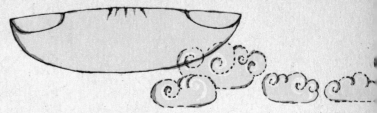

### YOUR EXTRA FINGER

You have an extra finger
floating around in the air.
How do you know?
Hold your two first fingers
a little in front of your eyes.
Look past them toward the wall.

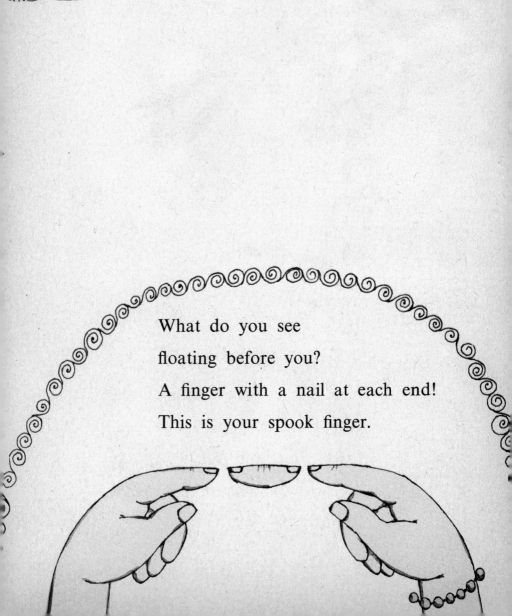

What do you see
floating before you?
A finger with a nail at each end!
This is your spook finger.

## PINCUSHION THUMB

Here is a trick to do for your friends.
Tell them, "I can stick pins in myself
because I am a spook."
Hold out your fist
   with the thumb pointing up.

Place a handkerchief over your thumb.

Stick a pin into your thumb.

Stick more pins into your thumb.

Then pull out the pins.

Take away the handkerchief and—

your thumb is unharmed!

The secret:

Hide a carrot in your fist.

Hold it up like a thumb.

When you take away the handkerchief,

hide the carrot in your fist again.

## SPOOKY HAND

Place your hand flat on the table.
Push a card under it.
Then push another card under it.
Do this until ten cards are under your hand.
Say the magic word, "Hocus-pocus,"
and slowly lift your hand.
The cards come up with your hand!

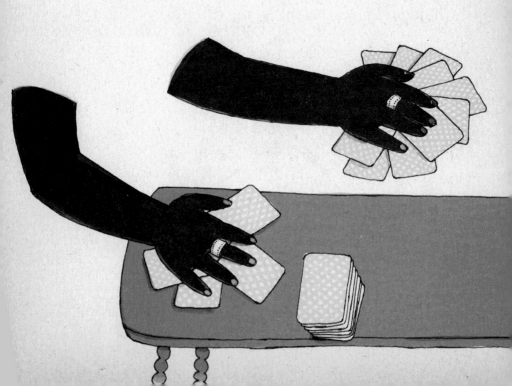

The trick:

Put on a ring.

Push a toothpick under it.

The toothpick holds the first two cards,

and they hold the others.

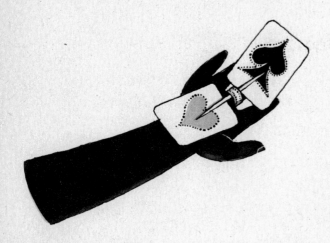

## STOP YOUR PULSE

Stick a match on a thumbtack.

Then set it on your wrist where the pulse beats.

At each beat, blood goes into your hand.

At each beat, the match shakes.

Say, "Hocus-pocus, pulse, stop,"

and the match is still.

Say, "Now I am dead. Start again, pulse."

The match starts shaking again.

"Now I am alive."

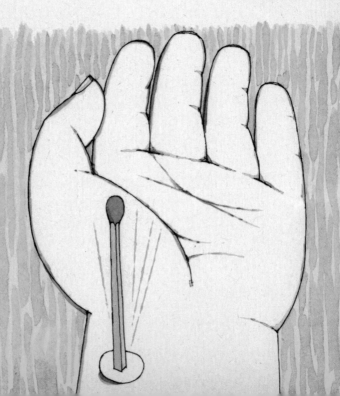

The trick:
Roll a handkerchief into a lump
and put it under your arm.
Press your arm against your side.
The lump presses against your arm
and stops the blood from going to your hand.

## Strange string

Say, "Only a spook can do this.

Here are two strings.

I will make them become one."

Put the upper ends into your mouth.

The other ends hang down.

Chew the string.

Make faces and roll your eyes.

Take hold of a hanging end and pull it.

Out comes the string in one long piece!

The secret:

Use one long string.

Loop it with a very short one.

Hide the loop with your thumb

(as in the picture on page 18).

Then put it into your mouth.

Keep the short string in your mouth.

Pull out the long one.

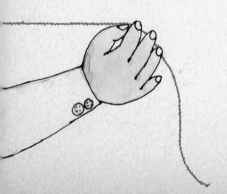

## Spooky handkerchief

Say, "My handkerchief is spooky like me.

A coin will pass through it."

Hold up a coin between your finger and thumb.

Cover it with your handkerchief.

Pinch the handkerchief

between your thumb and the coin.

Flip the handkerchief back

to show that the coin is still there.

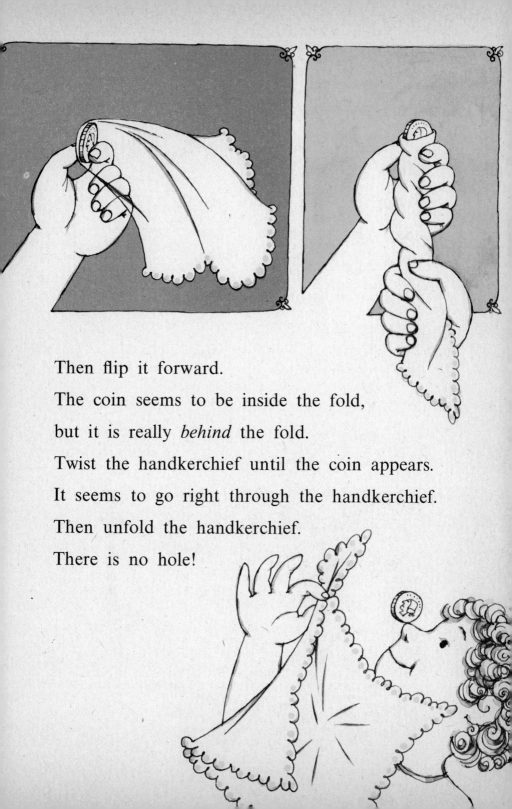

Then flip it forward.
The coin seems to be inside the fold,
but it is really *behind* the fold.
Twist the handkerchief until the coin appears.
It seems to go right through the handkerchief.
Then unfold the handkerchief.
There is no hole!

## Rising ring

Say, "My ring can move by itself.

It is spooky too."

Drop the ring over a pencil.

Say, "Hocus-pocus."

The ring slowly rises.

Then it falls and rises again.

The trick:
Take a black thread.
Tie one end to your coat button.
Fix the other end under the eraser.
No one will see the thread.
If you lean back, the thread pulls tight
and makes the ring rise.
Lean forward and the ring falls.

## X-RAY EYES

Tell your friends,
"I can see through things
with my X-ray eyes.
I can read through folded paper."

Have a pencil and a note pad ready.
Say, "Each person spell his name,
and I will write it down."
As each one spells his name
write on a sheet from the pad.
Fold each sheet and drop it into a bag.
When all are in the bag,
ask somebody to pick out a sheet.
Stare at the folded paper. Then say,
"I see that the name is John."
When the paper is unfolded,
the name on it is "John."

The trick:
Pick one name—suppose it is John—
and write that name on every sheet.

Tell your friends,
"When I go spooking,
I sometimes need a helper.
I have a good one.
My helper is a very small ghost.
His name is Willie.
Do you want to meet him?"

### WILLIE IN A MATCHBOX

Say, "Willie is so little.
He sleeps in a matchbox."

Lay the matchbox on your hand.
Say, "Willie, it's time to get up."
Slowly bend your fingers down.
The matchbox rises and stands up.
"Now it's bedtime. Go to bed, Willie."
Straighten your fingers,
and the box lies down.

The trick:
Place the matchbox
upside down on your hand.
Pinch a little skin
between the box and the cover.

## CREEPY COIN

Stand a glass upside down on two coins.

Place a dime between the coins.

Say, "Willie, bring the dime to me."

Scratch on the tablecloth

with your fingernail.

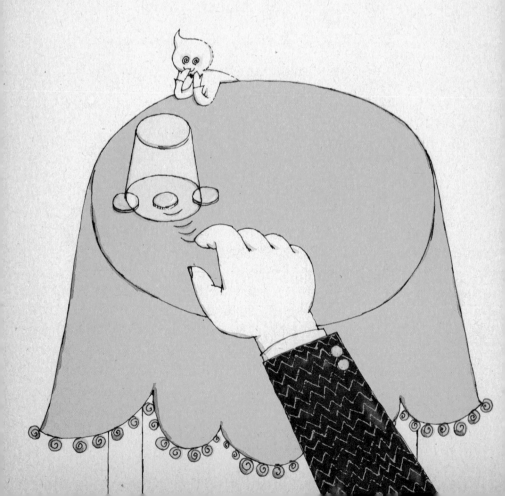

Scratch and scratch.
The dime comes out
from under the glass!
That is all you do.
The scratching moves the dime.

## WILLIE PLAYS BALL

Put a ball on the table and say,
"Willie likes to play ball.
Willie, give the ball a push."
As your friends watch
the ball moves back and forth.

The trick:

Tie a thread to a ring.

Place the ring under the tablecloth.

Run the thread over and under the tabletop.

Put the ball on the ring.

When you pull the thread,

the ring moves the ball.

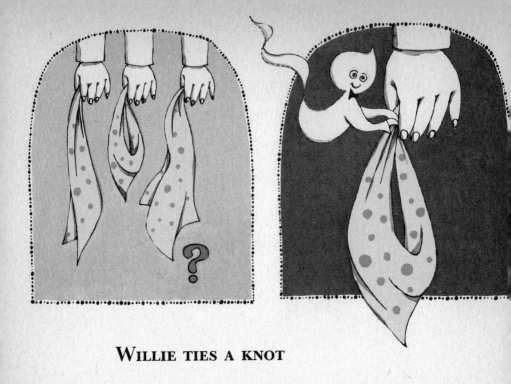

### WILLIE TIES A KNOT

Hold out a handkerchief by one corner.
Say, "I will tie a knot by magic."
Then lift the lower corner
and hold it in the same hand.
Flip the handkerchief
so it hangs down as before.
No knot appears. Too bad!
You try again. Still no knot appears.
"Oh dear!" you say. "I need Willie.
Willie, help me. Please tie a knot."

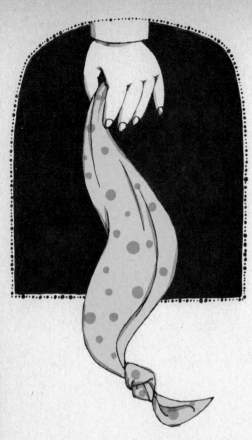

Flip the handkerchief once more and—
a knot appears in the lower corner!

The trick:
Tie a knot in one corner of the handkerchief.
Hold this corner so you hide the knot.
When you want the knot to appear,
let the knotted corner drop down.

## WILLIE EARNS A NICKEL

Say, "Willie, you are a good helper.

I will give you a nickel."

Rub the nickel on your sleeve and say,

"I must shine the nickel."

Drop the nickel and pick it up.

Rub it some more.

Hold out your hand and say,

"Here is your nickel, Willie."

Then show that your hand is empty.
Your other hand is empty too.
Willie took his nickel!

The trick:
When you drop the nickel,
pick it up with one hand.
Keep it there, but pretend
to shift it to the other hand.
Then hold out the empty hand.
As you do this, slip the nickel
into your shirt.

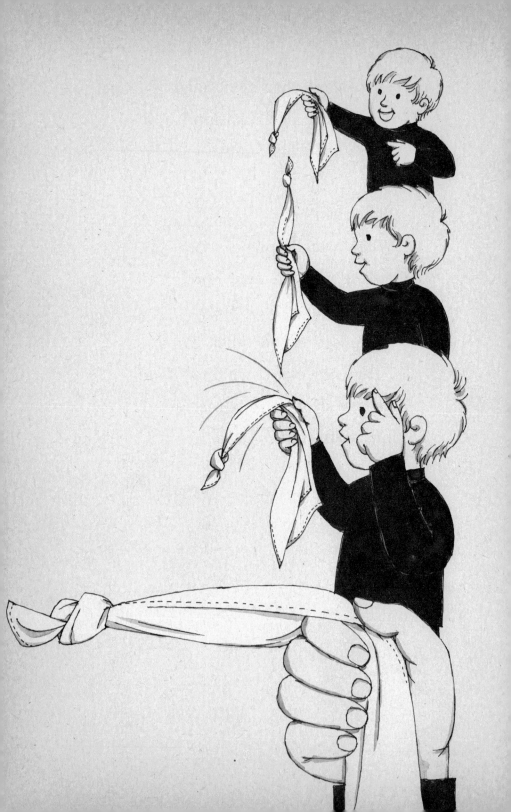

## WILLIE TAKES A BOW

Show a handkerchief
with a knot in one corner.
The knot hangs down in front of your hand.
Say, "This is Willie, the ghost.
He is hiding in my handkerchief.
Willie, see all the nice people."
Willie seems to hear you,
for the knot rises.
Say, "Bow to the people," and
the knot bobs up and down.

The trick:
Make a hole in the hem of the handkerchief.
Push a short piece of wire into the hem.
To make the knot bob up,
press the end of the wire with your thumb.

## CANDY FOR WILLIE

Hold up a paper cup
so the bottom rests on your palm.
Put a piece of candy in the cup.
Say, "This is for Willie, the ghost.
Willie, take your candy."
Cover the cup with a handkerchief.

Then uncover it
and turn the cup upside down.
The candy is gone.


The trick:

Make a hole in the bottom of the cup
so the candy drops into your hand.

41

# HAUNTED
# HOUSE

Say,

"Over this house I cast a spell.

Hocus-pocus, watch me well.

Hocus-pocus, watch and see

things as scary as can be.

Hocus-pocus, danger and doom!

Ghosts and spooks come into the room.

Haunt the house. Start the show.

Hocus-pocus—ready, let's go!"

## GHOST ON THE WALL

Draw a large picture of a ghost.
Make him black with white eyes.
Tell your friends to stare at the picture.
They stare at it for a minute.
Then tell them to stare toward the wall.
What do they see?
They see the ghost, but now he is white.
Their own eyes play a trick on them.

## MUMMY FINGER

Say, "What do I have in this box?
A mummy's finger
that I dug up in Egypt.
Do not faint, now."
Open the box.
It is packed with cotton.
Push aside the cotton and—
there is the mummy's finger!

The trick:
It is your own finger.
You poke it into the box
through a hole in the bottom.

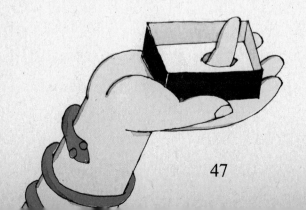

## ELECTRIC CAT

Show your cat and say,
"I had a spooky kitten
that became a spooky cat.
She sparkles in the dark.
Now what do you think of that!"
Turn out the lights.
The sparks jump up
around your spooky cat.

The trick:
Use a long-haired cat for this trick.
Run a comb through the cat's fur.
This charges the fur with electricity.

## SIGN OF THE SPOOK

Show a lump of sugar and a pencil.
Write the letter "S" on the sugar.
Then drop the sugar into a glass of water.
Say, "Sugar, melt. Letter 'S' float up."
Have a friend hold his hand over the glass.
Then tell him to look at his hand.
There on his palm is the "S."
It is the sign of the spook!

The trick:

Press your finger on the "S" on the sugar.

The "S" comes off on your finger.

When you show your friend what to do,
hold his hand and touch his palm
with your finger.

This puts the "S" on his palm.

## MIXED-UP MUMMIES

Show two matchboxes
and two paper-doll mummies.
One mummy is purple. The other is green.
Put the purple mummy in a box.
Mark the end of that box with a purple "X."
Put the green mummy in the other box.
Mark the end with a green "X."
Cover the boxes with a cloth.

Then uncover them and open them.

The mummies have changed places!

Before the trick, mark one end of each box.

Mark a green "X" on the purple mummy's box.

Mark a purple "X" on the green mummy's box.

Keep these ends out of sight.

As you uncover the boxes

turn them around so these ends show.

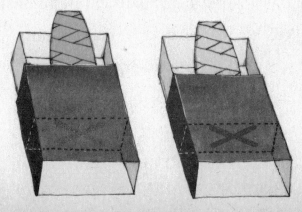

### Disappearing Girl

Show a large cardboard box and say,
"Will some brave lady please come here.
I will make her disappear."
A brave girl comes up.

Have her step into the box.

Put down the cover. Wave your hands
and say some magic words.

Then tip the box forward and lift the cover.

The box is empty!

This is how you fix the box:

Cut around the bottom on three sides.

Then bend the bottom toward the front.

Put a handle on the bottom.

When the girl steps into the box,

she is standing on the floor.

When you tip the box forward,
she pulls the bottom back.
When you lift the cover,
she is hidden behind the box.
How does the girl know what to do?
She practiced and practiced
the trick with you.

## FLOATING BOY

Say, "For my last and biggest surprise,

a boy will float before your eyes."

A low bench is ready. It is covered with a sheet.

Two helpers stand waiting.

Who will be the floating boy?

A friend comes up—suppose his name is John.

Have him stand behind the bench.

Your two helpers

take the sheet.

They hold it up

before the bench.

John is hidden behind the sheet.

He lies down on the bench.

The helpers cover him with the sheet.

Only his head and feet show.

Wave your hands over John.

Say, "Rise! Rise!"

And John floats up into the air!

The picture shows how the trick is done.
Two sticks with shoes on the ends
are hidden under the sheet.
When John lies down, he knows what to do.
He keeps his feet on the floor
and takes hold of the two sticks.
Then he slowly stands up.
As he stands he lifts the sticks.
Take off the sheet, and everybody laughs.

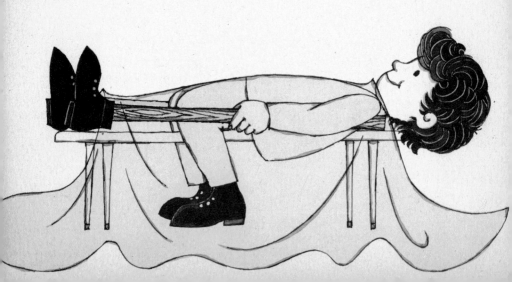

The spell is broken. The ghosts all go.

This is the **END** of the spooky show.